CAPTAIN COOL
AND THE ICE QUEEN

Cambridge Reading

General Editors
Kate Ruttle and Richard Brown

Consultant Editor
Jean Glasberg

PUBLISHED BY THE PRESS SYNDICATE OF THE UNIVERSITY OF CAMBRIDGE
The Pitt Building, Trumpington Street, Cambridge CB2 1RP, United Kingdom

CAMBRIDGE UNIVERSITY PRESS
The Edinburgh Building, Cambridge CB2 2RU, United Kingdom
40 West 20th Street, New York, NY 10011-4211, USA
10 Stamford Road, Oakleigh, Melbourne 3166, Australia

Text and illustrations © Gerald Rose 1998

First published 1998
Reprinted 1998

Printed in the United Kingdom by the University Press, Cambridge

Typeset in Concorde

A catalogue record for this book is available from the British Library

ISBN 0 521 55649 X paperback

Captain Cool
and the Ice Queen

Gerald Rose

CAMBRIDGE
UNIVERSITY PRESS

Captain Cool had sailed all around the
world.

Now he lived in an old boat that rested
on the mudflats of a wide river not far
from the open sea.

The *Merry May* was Captain Cool's pride
and joy. He was always mending bits here
and painting bits there, keeping everything
ship-shape.

The captain's only crew member was
Patch, the ship's cat.

5

Captain Cool loved to tell stories of his travels and adventures, but he told the same stories over and over again. His friends soon got bored with them.

One morning, Captain Cool woke up
feeling very damp. It had been raining
all night.

The captain pressed his nose to the porthole to look out at the rain. He couldn't believe his eyes! The river had risen and was lapping round his boat.

It rained all day and all night. Soon the river had risen so much that the boat began to float away.

The *Merry May* was swept out to sea and tossed about on the wild waves.

Before long, the rain turned to snow and the air grew icy.

Patch felt seasick. She stayed below deck
trying to keep out of the way of all the
things that were rolling and sliding around
the floor.

At bedtime that night, Captain Cool's cocoa froze into a lump in his mug. Icicles hung from the ceiling.

By the next morning, the wind had stopped, and the boat was surrounded by ice. The sea was freezing solid.

Soon the ship was locked in solid ice.
Captain Cool and Patch were amazed to see
an enormous iceberg towering above them.

This is very odd. We don't normally find icebergs around here.

I've never seen one like this, even in the Arctic.

It's more like a castle than an iceberg.

It was so strange and beautiful that they decided to go and explore.

They left the boat and climbed the slippery crags. They reached what looked like a path. But, suddenly, they came face to face with a fierce polar bear.

Quick as a flash, Captain Cool stepped forward, took hold of the bear, and threw it over his shoulder.

The path led them to an entrance. Inside,
strange noises echoed around them.
It sounded as if someone was laughing
at them.

Suddenly, Patch heard the sound of ice cracking above their heads.

They both leapt aside just in time as a huge icicle shattered at their feet. More icicles smashed around them. They started to run and . . .

they slipped on
the icy floor,
tumbling and
bouncing off
the walls.
Down, down,
down they fell.

CRASH!
It was a painful landing.

Before they had time to work out where they were, they were greeted by a loud and gleeful laugh . . . it was the Ice Queen!

The Ice Queen boasted of her evil plans.
To show her powers, she snapped her fingers, and . . .

suddenly, two large polar bears appeared
with a huge barrel of water. They poured it
over the side of the iceberg.

As the water touched the ground, the Ice
Queen blew an icy breath and left a
column of sparkling ice standing in the
freezing air.

The Ice Queen had more surprises for
Captain Cool. She snapped her fingers and
. . . a giant fiddler crab appeared.

The crab tried to grab the captain's hand
with his huge claw. (This fiddler was a little
too friendly for Captain Cool's liking.)

Captain Cool was glad that he was wearing his extra-strong string vest.

The vest unravelled easily, and Captain
Cool quickly used the string to make
a lasso.

After a few quick twirls, Captain Cool
dropped his lasso over the crab's giant
claw.

The Ice Queen was very angry.

She snapped her fingers and . . . suddenly, a giant squid appeared. She looked hungry and miserable.

Captain Cool just couldn't stop staring into the squid's hypnotic eyes.

The evil Ice Queen rushed forward and pushed him into the water!

37

Captain Cool was glad he'd been taught
lots of sailor's knots when he was a young
cabin boy. He grabbed some of the squid's
tentacles and tied them together.

This made the squid angry. She shot out clouds of black ink and jetted up and down the pool. She travelled so fast that she leapt out of the pool and . . .

landed right on top of the Ice Queen.

41

The giant squid wrapped her tentacles round the Ice Queen's neck.

43

In the confusion, Captain Cool picked up the queen's magic crown and ran.

They slid down the column of ice – it snapped just as their feet touched the ground.

It's just as well the queen showed us her ice-making trick! This column of ice is coming in handy.

If I'd wanted to spend my life sliding down slippery poles, I'd have joined the fire brigade.

The Ice Queen soon dealt with the slippery squid. She escaped from the squid's tentacles, twirled the squid above her head and tossed her back into the pool.

Then she punished the bears for letting Captain Cool steal her crown.

Snapping off spiky icicles as she went, the Ice Queen gave chase. She used the icicles as spears.

Captain Cool and Patch skilfully dodged
the shower of icicle-spears that fell around
them.

49

Slipping and sliding as fast as they could, they soon reached the boat.

Safely on board, Captain Cool turned on the stove and heated lots of water for a bath.

There's nothing like a good hot bath when you're feeling really cold.

He filled the bath and put in some bubble bath. He found a big, fluffy towel and his favourite duck.

The Ice Queen sped across the ice getting closer and closer. She carried a huge ice spear.

Captain Cool put on the crown and lay in his bath. He was covered in bubbles. The hot water made him turn pink.

The Ice Queen jumped onto the boat and looked down the hatch.

In a rage she dived towards the captain, straight into the bath.

SPLOOOSH! Great clouds of steam and
bubbles filled the cabin.

Captain Cool had managed to get out just
in time.

When all the steam and bubbles had cleared away, there was no sign of the Ice Queen. All that remained of her was a puddle of very cold water.

Now that the queen was gone, the iceberg-castle started to melt away. The frozen sea broke up and the captain was able to start up his engine.

Captain Cool couldn't wait to get back to the mudflats.

Now he had a new story to tell.

On hot summer days, Captain Cool would put on his magic crown and breathe out an icy breath.

The river would freeze to make a
wonderful skating rink. Captain Cool
served cold drinks, and there was never a
shortage of ice.